Gay Letters
From Millicent
to Maude

James Considere
&
Bill Edwards

GAY LETTERS FROM MILLICENT TO MAUDE

Printed in the United States of America

Cover and Book Graphics Design by:
Imagine It! Media
Palm Springs, CA
info@imagineitmedia.com

Cover Illustration by:
Jeffrey Kirby, Rancho Mirage, CA

Preface

Far more than uniquely witty individuals, Maude and Millicent were gay male debutantes and their charm and high spirit provide us with wonderful insight into gay culture, film icons and fashion of the 1950's; and Maude with his savior faire was surely put on this earth by God to cheer up Millicent and many, many other friends.

This work is dedicated to Hugh C.

[1]Colette was famous for breaking the rules of masculinity and femininity after the turn of the twentieth-century and for her brilliant writing (her first books were published pseudonymously under her bisexual husband's name) which includes "Gigi", but also for her performance at the Moulin Rouge in 1907 when she kissed a woman in front of a terror-stricken audience. She was considered so brazen that the police banned her revue and banned her and the woman with whom she was romantically involved with from living together.

Dear Maudine:

Saturday was so beautiful I spent the major part
of the day in Central Park reading Colette[1]. She is
so fabulous. Be sure to read her short novel
collections, 'Cheri' and 'The Last of Cheri'.

I started talking to a policeman (off duty) in the
park and we walked around. He bought me cracker-
jacks, and I felt just like Ginger Rogers again.

Of course, I knew I was playing with fire but I
sort of accidentally groped LILY LAW (I fully
expected him to tear my navy cashmere sweater to
shreds, but he sort of liked the attention).

In no time at all I had him on my sofa, and I
devoured him feathers and all. He did not want to
arrest me or anything and he said goodbye most
pleasantly. Like an idiot I gave him my real name
and phone number.

I may be resting peacefully in the Girls Detention
Home tomorrow, but I will deny everything and say
that he raped me.

Millie

[2]The hotel Elysee on E. 54th in Midtown New York was the home and hub of sophisticated New Yorkers (Tennessee Williams lived there until his death in 1983), world celebrities and Hollywood actors. The Monkey bar piano bar with its monkey-themed murals was a coveted, exclusive watering hole for the top names in town.

[3]Lillian Gish was very demure, always coiffed, and she always dressed for the occasion in New York City. She enjoyed her career that spanned decades in silent films, "the talkies" and stage and television. She had a leading role in the drama "The Night of the Hunter" released in 1955, and during the 1950's she also became a guest lecturer who still enthralled audiences with her theatrical presence and her love of the motion picture industry. She never married.

[4]The legendary bar at New York's Bon Soir in Greenwich Village was designed with ebony and white accents, was standing room only and was always crowded with sophisticated gay men. Round tables were scattered around the entertainment area. The patrons were 'swells' and were very courteous to the comedians, singers and musicians who performed sometimes for their first time.

Dear Maude:

Isn't this a wonderful time to live in New York City?

Lois Le Chance looked extremely demure at the Hotel Elysee[2] yesterday afternoon, but there we were seated with him and keeping company with Lillian Gish[3] at the Monkey Bar.

Darling, we always look so proper together in our cord jackets and gray flannels. And, don't we wander everywhere around this fabulous city of New York like a pair of Boston debutantes?

Bon Soir[4] is our place to shine at night, and we look so vibrant against its black and white decor.

Your fabulous sister,

Millie Le Coco

[5]By most accounts she was not a compelling actress, but Hedda Hopper's gossip columns played favorites and she could bring an actor or actress divine press or moralistic condemnation, especially if she thought one was left of center. It is reported that she tried to out actors Cary Grant and Randolph Scott as gay lovers. Hopper's arch-enemy until later years was columnist Louella Parsons, and the two ruled Hollywood until their authority faded as Hollywood's and America's morals changed.

Dear Maude:

For heaven's sake, you finally wrote to me. I did
not want to be forced to tell Hedda Hopper[5] about
that illegitimate child you had in Austria.

I have my summer play clothes out today for
inspection, just in case someone dares to invite me
to Newport for the season. Much to my dismay, I
find I can only last two days at the most with my
present garb. I think I will make a smart number
for the beach out of my old gray cashmere and put
a smart black leather belt and cuffs on it.

I met a rather nice, but a bit old guy accidentally.
He's with Texas Standard Oil. He took me to a movie and then to the most elegant place for cocktails
and dinner on Sunday evening. The restaurant bill
was outrageous.

I looked radiant. The management sent over creme
de menthe with their compliments after dinner. He
said it was because of my being so attractive and
charming, and I agreed.

I must keep in good with him until after Christmas.
You know how I adore wild mink. Throughout this I
have somehow miraculously managed to be trade and
I hope I won't be forced to mess up those wax lips
you gave me.

Love,

Millie

Maude:

What a lovely, clever Christmas card - it looked so
much like you - I suppose as we grow older we try
to bring back our youth as much as we can.

The old buzzard who gifted me a quart of Faberge -
well, his Christmas gifts were a bit more practical
- three huge, immense lovely towels (which must
have cost roughly $8 apiece), a dark blue cashmere
scarf and a pair of argyle socks (I loathe argyle).

The only sensible thing he bought for me was a
bottle of champagne. I was dead set on getting
a mink, but if you can't have mink then I say
cashmere is best.

Now, sweet, I am all goose pimples and white
ermine at the idea that you're going to powder
those sugar coated cookies in your basket and toot
on up to New York to visit.

Please don't wait until August as I hope to be
in a show by then.

Love,

Millie

Dear Maude:

I know it's the beginning of the horse jump
competitions and you are cleaning all of those
soiled jodhpurs, but we must not let our
correspondence lag.

I have begun the grind of sweating out eight
hours of work and then night class. Really,
it's the plight of the poor working girl.

Saturday, I had a rehearsal for this silly
ballet (put on by young choreographers) I am
performing in without a costume. We only had
the theatre for an hour and only had time to
run through the ballet once with an orchestra,
our one and only orchestral rehearsal. We
rehearsed on Sunday for four hours and then
I dashed home and then it was back to the theatre.

On with the slap (theatrical makeup) and there I
was camping on the stage like crazy. I did have a
couple of grand jetes alone and a few high kicks
and I put my heart and soul into
this bit. I was sexsational.

All my love,

Millie

[6]Paulette Goddard reportedly was a top candidate to play the role of Scarlet O'Hara in "Gone with the Wind", but the marital inconsistencies concerning her and Charlie Chaplin reportedly caused David O. Selznick to instead cast Vivien Leigh for the role of Scarlet. Goddard became a New York socialite and was a friend with Andy Warhol.

[7]When asked if she had ever studied acting or singing Dorothy Lamour said, "No, can't you tell?" She became famous for her print sarong wrap-around in "The Jungle Princess" and continued the same prop in the numerous "Road" pictures with Bob Hope and Bing Crosby.

Dear Paulette Goddard[6]:

Pet, when I arrived home last night and started
unpacking my dance bag and suddenly spied your
letter on the table, you should have seen my living
room floor - toe shoes, mesh opera hose and eyelash
beading all thrown helter-skelter.

If I thought I should never have another letter
from you I would slit my wrists with that lovely,
old Queen Anne letter opener.

My life has been about as exciting as those poor
old sheep that graze around Buda, Texas.

I have given up the rather rich Esso Oil mess. At
the last tete-a-tete I showed about as much emotion
as Dorothy Lamour[7] - need I say it didn't go over
so well. I just couldn't go through with it so I
just left rather hurriedly.

I shall miss all the elegant lobster and steak din-
ners; and that quart of Faberge has dwindled so
quickly, but that is fate, or a queen's indulgence.

The "Can-Can" audition is over and done with, or
did I tell you. I stayed on until the last twenty.
"Carnival in Flanders" comes up next week and I
shall diligently put my best leg forward again.

As ever,

Millie

[8]Lana Turner was an MGM actress who starred in "The Postman Always Rings Twice" and her off-stage life took somewhat of a film noire turn when in 1958, her daughter, Cheryl Crane, fatally stabbed Turner's shady boyfriend, Johnny Stompanato. Crane acted in self-defense. The movie, "LA Confidential", 1997, recreates a memorable restaurant dining scene with Lana Turner and Johnny Stompanato at West Hollywood's Formosa restaurant. Turner received a nomination for Best Actress in "Peyton Place" and she starred in "Imitation of Life" and "Madame X" among many films.

[9]A disturbed Blanche DuBois, portrayed by Vivien Leigh in "A Streetcar Named Desire", was Vivien Leigh's second Oscar. Her first Oscar was "Gone with the Wind". In her later years, Leigh became a manic-depressive. She died at the age of 53 from tuberculosis. Jessica Tandy also portrayed the character of Blanche on stage.

Maude, my love:

If I thought I should never receive another
letter from you I'd hang myself this very
instant with a black chiffon scarf. I positively
adore you.

Did I tell you I had a long distance call from Ms.
Hanks last week? What a harlot. She is so fruity
(and I despise that word) she makes a fruit cake
look straight.

Does she come by to see you? I suppose by now she
is old and wrinkled or does the AC-DC bit keep one
young? I have a feeling that her wife (who is
really Lon Chaney in drag) will get the goods
on that lady one of these days and watch out.

That wife is so vindictive she will put dried fruit
in his burial niche.

I suggest you drop the bitch.

C'est a la crumpet. It is lunch time, and I
must powder my nose and snake hip all the way
to the cafeteria. I do wish they would have
vichyssoise just once. I am so sick of cottage
cheese and salad I could croak. But then again
I am not Lana Turner[8].

As Ever,

Blanche Du Bois[9]

[10]French dolls were quite expensive, but they
became unfashionable at some point after the
1950's. Today, some consider them to be de rigueur
and they are actively collected and sold on
E-Bay and auction houses.

Dearest Maude:

I am giving a small tea dance this weekend.

You could whiz up here in your little beige Jaguar
and look resplendent in your cocoa dyed ermine and
that little pillbox hat full of iridescent sequins.

Please bring Ms. Parry along in her sweet yellow
corduroy jumper. Is she still on the swing shift at
that cafeteria?

I have embroidered a new skirt for the French
doll[10] on your bed. Her name is "Nellie". Everyone
used to have life sized French dolls on their bed,
darling.

I am trying to get my friend, Lolly, to come down
here for a visit, too. She is so fabulous that I
feel she could absolutely wreck Neiman Marcus.

Love,

Millicent

[11]A luxurious Isotta-Fraschini was driven by the butler/chauffeur, Max, (Erich von Stroheim) in "Sunset Boulevard" starring Gloria Swanson and William Holden. These exotic Italian cars were also owned by movie stars Rudolph Valentino and Clara Bow. The Isotta-Fraschini was discontinued in 1949.

[12]Carole Landis was reportedly born into poverty, dropped out of high school, but she was bound for Hollywood. She was cast by producer Hal Roach in her film breakthrough, "One Million B.C.", which landed her the female role as a cave woman. Her career suffering and several marriages dissolved she began dating actor Rex Harrison who was married at the time. It is said that when he refused to divorce his wife, Carole tragically committed suicide by an overdose. Her family denies her suicide and claims her death to have been murder.

My Darling Maude:

That scathing duel fought over you by the duke and
the count. Oh dear, when I think of you now riding
throughout Austria in the duke's Isotta-Fraschini[11].

Remember when we used to hitch-hike rides in
Austria.

When I think of those days I want to commit
a Carol Landis[12]. There were so many, many
opportunities and so much meat available.

Really, my dear, why didn't you enlighten me when
we were there?

I really want to see you. Maybe we can get
together somewhere and camp. Do you think we
are too matronly to go to Mineral Wells for a
week and take the baths?

As always,

Millie

[13]In 1953, Henry Cabot Lodge, Jr. rose from the ranks of U.S. Senator of Massachusetts to become the U.S. ambassador to the United Nations. He was distinguished looking and came with a prestigious family name in culture and politics. He was a moderate Republican.

[14]Andrew Geller shoes (pumps and loafers) were the popular choice of women's office fashion in the 1950's. They were considered comfortable for the office and reputable in quality. The company is still in operation today.

Dear Maude:

I have been busier than a stitch queen at Mardis Gras.

I have no social life (the A-group here insists I am too old to be a debutante). I have no love life or money either and that's three things a southern belle must have.

Maude, I am terribly in love with Henry Cabot Lodge[13]. I wrote him a letter of admiration and asked for a picture, but there has been no answer as of yet.

Don't you think he is terribly attractive? So polished - oh my dear, green grows the lilacs.

I pray to the Lord that Henry Cabot will come charging after me at the office, and I will never have to face a typewriter or a pair of Andrew Geller[14] shoes again.

I know that right now you are dripping in pastel chiffons.

Write soon.

Millicent

[15]Known as the dancer in the Old Gold cigarette box, Dixie Dunbar was a New York City dancer brought to The Great White Way by her mother who recognized Dixie's dancing talent as a child in Alabama. "I enjoyed my career, but it was my mother who had all the ambition", she remarked. Her first film at age 16 was "Scandals" in 1934. She danced in up market night clubs and restaurants. After several movies she became disillusioned with film and later joined up with Buddy Ebsen, Phil Silvers and Judy Canova on Broadway. Her last marriage was to a millionaire from Miami Beach.

Dear Dixie Dunbar[15]:

Your letter certainly helped to make an
impossible weekend more bearable.

I know you are busy with your Winter Cotillions
and your Junior League work, but really doll, just
scribble me a line often even if you must write it
on your dance program.

Virginia Harold dashed by Saturday. She read your
letter and went into a slight case of hysterics.
We went to dinner, and after dinner we sailed into
Glennon's for drinks.

We both saw what we liked at Glennon's, but we
couldn't get it. We're so elegant and proper
we just won't begin conversations with total
strangers.

I heard that Cinderella Gillin breezed back to New
York after almost six months of living in Texas.
He met a boy from "Paint Your Wagon", fell madly
in love and then followed him to New York. Maude,
that girl loses her head at even the slightest
provocation

Millicent

[16]Dorothy Kilgallen was a New York syndicated gossip columnist and celebrity panelist on the favorite 50's television show, "What's My Line". She was found dead 12 hours after her last "live" appearance on the show which ran from 1950 to 1967. There was speculation over her death and whether there was a connection to conspiracies raised in her syndicated column about the Kennedy assassination while other speculation raises issues of a drug and alcohol overdose, or an accidental overdose. The cause of death was "undetermined". Before her death Frank Sinatra became annoyed with her and he intermittently made comments referring to her as the "chinless wonder".

[17]British author, Charlotte Bronte, pseudonymously wrote "Jane Eyre" under the pen name of Currer Bell. The Gothic novel about an orphan was set in the Yorkshire Moors and reproduced on a Hollywood stage by Twentieth Century Fox. The original movie was released in 1944 starring Orson Wells and Joan Fontaine with a non-credited role by the young Elizabeth Taylor. A new film was produced and released in March, 2011.

[18]Ginny Simms was the lead singer with the Kay Kyser Orchestra. She had long white teeth, and with hair immaculately curled she would sit in a chair between her performances until her next introduction by Kay Kyser. She died in Palm Springs, California in April, 1994.

Dear Maude:

I could not resist forwarding you the
following:

Lois Le Chance made Dorothy Kilgallen's[16] column in
New York today, and I know that Lois is absolutely
delirious with all of this adulation and attention.

Miss Kilgallen said, quote: "Joan B. is very
excited about Tom Le Chance, a well-heeled Texan,
so socialite crowd says". Of course, they misspelled
her name in the actual column, but I am sure she
will not notice it. Now, please go out and buy some
honey for Ms. Le Chance's hot cross buns.

You horrid little slut, why haven't you written?

As ever,

Charlotte Bronte[17]

P.S. Louella Parsons asked me if it is true that
you are planning to do "The Ginny Simms Story"[18]
on TV. She said for you to let her know immediately because she has a damn "Exclusive" deadline.

Maudine:

I am aging and I feel every day of my twenty-four
years, but now that I am through with Hollywood it
really doesn't matter.

I suppose I have burned my candle at both ends
in New York and Texas.

I do miss New York City. Lord, how I miss the
city! I could cry every time I think about Bon Soir,
Schraffts, queens, Brooks, oh why!

Honey, the Texas heat is on here, and it just scares
me to wear my long white gloves to town. I still
say they are not ostentatious.

It is so hard to be the last civil war debutante in
this town.

Fort Worth continues to be the sheer essence of
boredom. Two of the semi-jolly bars have been
raided by the police and padlocked. They were just
"joints" anyway, and I always felt cheap slinking
into them.

Love,

Millie

Dearest Maudine:

Dallas is all right if you have producing oil wells
and I don't.

The queens are so piss elegant here. They run in
groups of three and turn their heads on you just
like you're a common whore.

All of the mad queens from Fort Worth run to
Dal-ass on Saturday night.

Well, honey, I am known in Paris, New York City
and Centerville, Texas, and I can be just as regal
as these Dallas queens pretend to be.

I do miss New York City and HOW. Like Mehitabel,
I am a city cat and these wide open spaces are too
damn wide.

I wish you would pack a box lunch and come
see me. We could finish that quilt we started.

Love,

Millie

New York City

"Happiness is a thing with lights"

-Millicent

Dear Maude:

The other day I called Louella Parsons. I asked,
"Honey, is Maude in Hollywood for a comeback?"

I had heard that you and several of the ladies
of the early talkie era were pulling in their
stomachs after a quick trip to that quack place in
Florida.

Louella could not say for sure about your
whereabouts, but she had heard through her butch
daughter, Harriet, that you are in Las Vegas
working as a hostess in some joi-pardon club.

Please let me know if you have any plans to visit
the land of disenchantment here so I can dash out
for a lesson in baking perfect chocolate souffles,
a favorite of yours.

All my love,

Millie

Dear Maude:

I do wish you would put away your scrap books and write to me. It's good to remember your days in the theatre, but sweetie, please don't continue to make a career out of it.

I still remember your days in New York. You took the town apart pulling off your shoes on Fifth Avenue (at the Plaza yet) and subsisting on nothing, but martinis and French onions.

Well, my life has just been through another crisis. Last Saturday, lard ass . . . excuse me, George spent the weekend in town. My cousin, Nini, called me around 4 p.m. and asked if I would like to come to a chic cookout and bring along George.

That was fine, although I had anticipated some expensive French cuisine for later that evening.

After changing from basic black to shorts and madras we went to Nini's cookout.

Well, at the cookout there was this person who took an instant dislike to me because of my charm and personality. We had some choice, cutting remarks.

Then George mentioned casually that he was a stockholder of a large bank in Texas after it crept into the conversation somehow. Well this same person's eyes lit up like a Broadway switchboard. During the evening she kept up a steady stream of chit chat with George, and that dumb ass ate it up. You

might say that I was ignored, and that doesn't sit
too well with me, especially at a cookout.

Finally, I picked up my cigarettes, dark glasses and
stalked out of the patio, daring the ivy to trip me.

I was so furious I went home and put out
cigarettes in a good jar of cold cream.

Love,

Millie

[19]It was a political belief in the 1950's that there were homosexual nests in Washington, D.C. that posed blackmail risks and subversive threats to American national life including a risk of sexual perversion of American youth. Conservative tabloids and politicians went on the attack. It was rumored that presidential candidate Adlai Stevenson, a wealthy divorced Democrat, was gay. He lost the 1952 presidential race to Republican candidate Dwight Eisenhower. It is reported that the Republicans ran a campaign of "Let's Clean House" to rid the government of communists and homosexual infiltration.

Dearest Maude:

These friends have wanted me to meet a certain
history teacher. I have declined because I find
teachers always try to bore me with facts, and as
you well know I have made history myself in my
days. After all, I gave Adlai[19] his campaign slogan
(Be Gay with Adlai), and where would Henry Cabot
Lodge be without my encouragement.

Well, Sunday night these friends had a little "do",
and I went over there for dinner. The teacher
proved to be a rather Nordic type and not too
disappointing. After dinner there was dancing, and
it was then I realized that there was an awful lot
of coffee in Brazil, need I say more. We rushed
back to my apartment. I won't go into the gruesome
details, but never have I ever seen such perfect
structure of a coffee table leg.

Tonight we are having a chic candlelight dinner
together complete with wine and Oregon pears.

Love,

Millicent

Ms. Maudine:

Forgive me for being late with my Easter
Greeting.

I had such a ghastly Easter. It rained and
everything was very wet. My pink organdy hat
with the cabbage roses and yellow streamers just
wilted and I was a Mess.

I finally had to give up on the hat and I wore that
old Milan sailor hat that you gave me. I goosed
it with a bit of glitter and everyone said I looked
"sweet". That wasn't the adjective I wanted to hear.

Lois the Lovely is playing hostess to poor queens.
She was so sweet to me while mother was here. We
had dinner with her, we attended a soiree at la
belle Gish's and of course, Easter morning we
drank champagne together.

Lois also gave me a huge bottle of cologne, and
needless to say I've upset the dressing room
like a black ostrich feather.

Write me soon, you foolish whore!

Millie

Dear Maude:

The curtain rang down last Sunday to the dullest
summer yet.

I threw my things in Mother's old Dodge, and it is
back to Death Valley. My dear, tell me this is all
a bad dream.

Just what I'm planning to do this fall remains to
be seen. The Count wants me to come back to Paris,
but I do not have the patience to manage a castle
and I hate all those stairs.

Ms. H. leaves for Europe in September. Let's give
that queen a hand - knowing her, she'll fuck her
way right through Her Majesty's Coldstream Guards!

Do they still haul people off to Newgate
prison?

Love,

Millie

[20]Rochelle Hudson was an actress who played the mother of Natalie Wood's character in "Rebel Without a Cause", a James Dean's breakthrough movie in 1955 that also starred Sal Mineo and Natalie Wood. She was also in "She Done Him Wrong" and received the memorable line from Mae West: "When a girl goes wrong, men go right after her". She died in the Palm Springs community of Palm Desert in 1972.

[21]German born Marlene Dietrich was an international sensation. When she came to America 'Mar-lay-na' was already the star at Paramount. Her American debut movie, "Morocco", featured her kissing a woman and wearing a man's formal white tail and tux. She was harmoniously of both sexes although she remained married to the same man her entire life. "In Europe it doesn't matter if you're a man or a woman" she once said. "We make love with anyone we find attractive"*. She valiantly entertained the allied enlisted men in World War II and performed for them playing a large saw with great accomplishment. It is said that she never performed for the officers, and she had to sometimes entertain on a cardboard floor erected over a muddy field. She was made an honorary colonel for her dedication. In the 1950's she became a stellar stage entertainer.
*Page 49, "A Legend's Last Years", People, 6/1/92

Dear Rochelle Hudson[20]:

My Las Vegas, Nevada trip was a glorious three day
vacation of sunning, drinking and wishing.

Harry Bellafonte's show was there, but the Marlene
Dietrich[21] show was the purpose of my trip. The
show was fabulous, if you pardon the expression.
Louella Parsons said Marlene brought Christmas
to Las Vegas.

The costumes! She changed from a gown of yellow
diamonds to a trailing coat of yellow Coq
feathers to a complete switch in white top hat
and tails. And then she sang, of all things,
"I've Grown Accustomed to Her Face".

Pet, I am working my butt off in Texas. I have no
social life.

Dallas is very HOT if you get the idea, and so I
have been staying in pressing flowers and small
birds.

Love,

Millicent

Dear Maudine:

There is no more Schraffts and no smart Madison
Avenue - so if things are not buzzing in Texas by
the end of summer I am simply going to have to
leave.

I can always go back to Paris and model for
Givenchy. You are sensible, in your hat selection
anyway, and I would just adore your advice as to
what I should do in this situation.

Well, last night by intuition (I can find a gay bar
anywhere) I went to a friendly looking bar called
JIM'S and it was gayer than purple galoshes.

I was so butch you would have thought I was Tab
Hunter. I played their shuffleboard machine, and I
did so well I even won a bottle of beer.

This sent my stock way up, and I pranced to the
juke box with roving eyes in my direction. In
general, I put a little life in the somewhat dismal
place.

About two blocks after leaving the bar, a black car
pulled up beside me at a red light. I recognized the
blonde driver as also having been in the bar. He
said with-out one trace of shame, "How about sex?"

I was too shocked; of course, to say anything, but
"Yes", and to insure my social standing in this
depressing town I gave a magnificent
performance.

Incidentally, I had a note from Ms. Parry.

He said he saw you before you packed all of those strapless things for your trip to Mexico and that you were thinking of joining up with a mariachi band. I want to know all of the details when you return, and I do mean details kosher, or non-kosher.

All my devotion,

Millicent

Dear Maude:

Just because I told Hollywood that you ran a small
cat house on West 75th in New York City is no
reason for you to get mad and ignore me.

The air here is getting the best of your sweet,
errant sister. Am I getting old?

I went to Toonerville Manor for the Thanksgiving
holiday. It was great to relax there and to have
some time alone to work on my memoirs.

Driving home do you know there was not one single
hitch hiker to be found? I was livid. I had made
several box lunches for a small picnic in some
secluded roadside park.

I brought home all my water colors from finishing
school, and I intend to do lots of creative things
for my little hut I intend to build on Padre Island.
I'm making it out of old beer cans and Mission wine
bottles.

Now that Ms. Roger is a hair burner I hope you are
setting up a little shop with her. I suppose you
are the Keeper of the Tweezers. Mary, whatever
happened to that bottle of Max Factor cologne we
had on the train?

I saw Joan Crawford emote all over the place in
"Autumn Leaves" - it's the story of all of our
mixed up lives. There's also a little scene you
might enjoy - the queen who plays her husband is

shown walking towards the camera in blue jeans,
no shirt and apparently not even a band aid
underneath. Maude, where did you put that old rat?
My dear, I am so lonely and miserable. I need the
bright lights, a little excitement, some new gowns
and a sentimental lover.

Please stop weaving those elaborate place mats
you're making for Christmas gifts and write.

Millie

Dear Maude:

You cheap purple glass bead queen. I had a
feeling you were at home sulking in that old
French beret because Grace Kelly didn't ask you
to be a bridesmaid.

Dallas is still such a bore, but I have managed to
corrupt most of the traveling salesmen from Maine
to Buda, TX. I have them before the Dallas piss
elegant queens in their Arrow shirts can come on
to them like cheap quicksilver.

In my heart, I feel I should return to New York,
but I have decided to be practical and stay in
Texas. Maybe I will rope a cowpoke and settle down
to raise dachshunds.

What men I have had here though are sadly in need
of a good sex education. Mary, there's more to it
than eating a piece of stuffed celery. Don't you
dare tell my grandmother that I ever said such a
thing like this to you!

Love, please write at once.

Millie

Dear Maudine:

I just looked at a former snapshot of you, and I
believe you were selling cigarettes at the Lido.
I guess we all had our day, Kid!

Honey, this place is for the birds, and I don't mean
swans. The habitues of the bars are provincial and
a bit on the seedy side. You know how I am about
the well-scrubbed look. In the dark, I guess they're
all the same.

One night in Dallas I ran face to face with a
person who was down from Houston to see Connie
Bennett's act. He said he was with people and
could not get away. He implored me to come to
Houston, and he gave me his telephone number.
It was probably the number of the Salvation
Army anyway. Queens are so cruel.

There is just NOTHING to do here, and I haven't got
the patience or time to muscle my way into the top
grade set.

I feel I am a bit advanced at that sort of
snobbery. After all, my dear, I have been to
bed with two titles.

Do write something kicky.

Millie

Dear Maude:

Your priceless letter (well, aren't they all?) has
been read, re-read and shared. Needless to say it
has brought gales of laughter into many jaded faces
that have refused to smile because of acquiring a
new wrinkle.

Maude, these dismal queens are all dying to meet
you, and you must come up some long weekend.

After classes, I motored to Mineral Wells as
planned. Child, I can't tell you exactly where it
is because my education in map reading is rather
limited, and you know I have absolutely no sense
of direction.

The country is quite beautiful and it does not look
like Texas at all. As soon as I got to the Springs
I had a bath and a good massage. It left me all
aglow and tingly and young again.

After resting I had tea and well you know Fate.
There was a very tall Texas gentleman with his
wife who was having a bit of nourishment.

He was very nice looking and he was dressed
in typically Texas summer fashion in a very
expensive sport shirt and brown slacks.

Suddenly, I felt he was paying more attention to me
than he certainly was to his wife. I returned his
glances in a coy manner (thank God I bought that
bottle of Murine and my eyes were soaked to the
gills.

Shortly, he came over and greeted me like a long
lost friend, called me Bob and introduced me to his
wife. This sort of shook me, but I played along.
Before I knew it I answered his question as to what
room I was in. It was strange, but I thought the
safest thing for me to do was to get to my room at
once and put on some more perfume. There was a
knock, and I knew damn well it wasn't room service.
Well, Maude, it was wilder than Billy Graham. And,
it left me weak and delicate as a new born calf.

After this pleasant, but not unexpected surprise I
dressed and had dinner at the Baker. I had a few
beers later, but I did not attempt to push Fate any
further. Anything else would have been a letdown.

Tell me more - when, where and how. I am so de-
lighted for you. I just wish I had someone beautiful, young, rich, virile and kind to care about me.
But alas, I suppose I'll just go on "by myself, with
myself, alone" as the song goes.

Love,

Millicent

Dear Maude:

It is so hot here.

Oh yes, I must tell you that I had a note from Lois
Le Chance. She merely gave me her itinerary for
the past year which consisted of Sutton Place, all
of Europe, Florida, Texas and Fire Island.

Several years ago in Europe she said she attended
the coronation. I wonder if she wore the same
attire as she did at Victoria's. But she had
broadened some since then.

Love,

Millie

Dear Maudine:

Mother bought me a new Ford yesterday. It is nothing pretentious. It is the cheapest model made in a bright vile blue.

There is no makeup bar, but there is adequate room in the trunk for packing crinolines and hatboxes.

I had a long, lengthy letter from Lolly Wilson, my old dancing school chum, and that girl has made history. Lolly did a very big movie star as trade, and the star loved it. Lolly is still floating on a cloud of pink rosebuds after that conquest.

I told you I was surprised to hear from Lois Le Chance since I left New York. She was a bit cool to me before I left. All right so I don't know how to tackle an artichoke broiled in lemon butter.

Write to me at once.

I have got to stop and get these French Braids fixed.

Millie

Dear Maude:

After having a drink at "Adolphus" the other
evening I decided to slink over to "Bandbox", a new
fabulous hangout. As I was making a grand and
sweeping entrance, a queen yelled out, "Hello
Millie, darling".

I almost jumped out of my smoked grey chiffon when
it turned out to be our Pauline Parry. I thought
she was still trying to model those junior dresses
at Sakowitz, but she has been transferred here, and
she is the belle of the house coat department at
Sears and Roebuck, or whatever.

She has been screwing everything in Dallas, and in
fact it took her three days to report to Sears with
a clear head. She has always had hot pants.

She is driving around in her copper Pontiac all
dolled up like a hairdresser on vacation. She
is wearing every wristwatch and ring in her
collection.

Please do write.

Millicent

Dear Maudine:

I thought you would like a note to have when you arrived home from Mexico. You always loved to open mail with those Jungle Red fingernails. Are they still that long?

I have been invited to Los Angeles to teach ballet, but what if the people don't like me. You know few ballet teachers teach in 5-inch heels. If I lived my life over I would have never left New York City.

New York City was fabulous, wasn't it, and weren't we, too. Very few people could sit stylishly on 5th Avenue and remove their shoes and get away with it.

Honey, your sister has a partial plate to replace those two teeth Grace Kelly kindly removed from me when the Prince showed he preferred me. I thrive on dentists.

Mae, why don't you drive up here and spend a weekend with me? There is not much to do, but we could camp and drink cokes. They are enlarging the highway here, and we could have some of the boys over for tea.

Love,

Millie

[22]Hedy Lamarr was an MGM actress. She was both gorgeous and a mathematical genius and inventor. Tandelayo in "White Cargo" was one of her memorable characters. She left MGM in 1945 and married W. Howard Lee, a Texas oil man, in 1953. They lived in Houston's up market River Oaks.

Dear Maudine:

I understand that you have come out of your
reclusion.

I know that you aren't making silent movies any-
more, but that's no sign for you to stay home and
to burn candles for Rudolph Valentino. One must
live life to the fullest before one gets all cozy in
a pine box in Band Aid, Texas.

I also understand that you and Hedy Lamarr[22] are
swapping jewelry and perfume like mad in Houston's
River Oaks. You have always loved perfume.

Please send me that number Hedy wore in "White
Cargo" for Halloween. That was her most famous
role. I am sure W. Howard Lee keeps her well.

I went to church this Sunday. The choir of Good
Shepherd sings like nightingales. It always
reminds me of the church wedding I never had.

As ever,

Millie

[23]Yma Sumac was an exotic Peruvian soprano with an extraordinary voice who sang songs of her native country and also performed Incan folk songs. Her career spanned several decades including popular lounge songs in the 50's and a techno dance recording, "Mambo Confusion" in 1971 that was played at euro-techno clubs.

Dear Maude:

No, my love, you have not been banished to
Siberia - just eliminated from The Goose Creek
Social Register. Since your letter arrived I
will register you next year.

Your letter hit the door step and I just cried. I
read it aloud to all the starlets and they just
roared as much as I did. Of course, I am sure they
did not understand a word of our doubletalk - it's
so confusing to write in both French and German.

Your new lover sounds devastating. Oh Maude, I am
so glad you are gay again. I believed you could
be if you just tried. Honey, don't sign any
papers and let him pay the rent. That's good
advice my Grand'Mere gave me years ago before I
left Le Havre. She was very French.

The other night in my wanderings, I met a man from
Brownwood, TX and it was real wild. I didn't know it
had swept the country like that. I proceeded to go
through my usual number in my same detached way,
but before you could say, "Bright Red Sequin" I was
behaving like a Roman goddess.

I am driving again and it's so wild, especially
repairing those Pierce Arrow coupe fenders. Write
me soon. I bet you are dripping in strapless, pink
chiffon tea dresses.

Love,

Yma Sumac[23]

Dear Bebe Daniels[24]:

Thank you for your letter. I know how old actresses in retirement are about writing. Surprisingly enough, your letter was quite legible. Louella Parsons mentioned you had a bit of palsy.

I do hope you will bring out the old plume hat and crank up the Duisenberg and motor over to Dallas for the weekend. Bring all the rhinestone collars you want.

George had a fit about my MG order (no, sweet you do not know him). He is real, and he is wild about your mother. And, he is practical, generous and kind. He is on the level, and he worries about me and the decisions I might be making.

He is reeking in money. Imagine, I think he is trying to make an honest woman out of me and at my age.

I think that this might mean a trip to Europe in April.

He thinks the MG purchase is impractical and I would be unhappy with it. Anyway, this was said over a very tasty lobster (he does take Millie to swell feeds). He does not want me to visit New Orleans either.

I will not let him screw up the MG deal and the New Orleans trip no matter what the certain consequences might be. Now, Maude, my pet, have you sufficiently recovered from this jolt?

To top the whole thing off, and what makes the whole thing so absolutely ridiculous is that I am his first fling of this sort. Maude, I am not lying.

Dear, I have been thinking that we could be a sensation in Biloxi? I have heard that it is very gay there.

Do you still have that polka-dot Chili Williams[25] swim suit?

Love,

Ann Harding[26]

[24]Bebe Daniels rode the wave of musicals until they faded from popularity. She starred in "Rio Rita" which was the hit movie of 1929. Radio Pictures dropped her contract, but still a draw she was then picked up by Warner Brothers' studio. In the 1933 comedy musical, "42nd Street", she delivered the quote: "Now go out there and be so swell that you'll make me hate you". She retired from pictures in 1935.

[25]Chili Williams was a blond model in the 1940's and the stunning 'polka-dot bikini' girl. She may have been the number one pin-up girl of the American armed forces in World War II.

[26]Ann Harding had distinctive elocution and talent for 'the talkies' and she had great success, but her career dwindled in the late 30's. She returned to film making later in "Eyes in the Night" and "The Man in the Gray Flannel Suit". She retired from acting in 1965 after performing in the hit television medical drama, "Ben Casey".

Dear Maude:

I had a frightening indiscretion the other night.
There was no place to go but to a lover's lane in a
secluded spot in a park.

Just as I was adjusting all those plastic flowers
on that smoked gray chiffon a car drove up and
darling, you can bet it was not an MGM talent
scout. Yes, it was LILY LAW. I was petrified and
wanted to scream, but something told me to not get
flustered and to just look natural.

I fluffed my flat top and answered yes to Lily's
questions - did I own the car, where did I buy it
and did I live in the area.

They left and I was trembling like a willow tree.
I know that they tagged my car and may tell my
employer. I guess I will have to begin cruising in
my English bicycle.

Love,

Millicent

Pet:

You mad, desirable empress! It was so good to talk
with you the other evening.

The New Orleans jaunt with you did wonders for me.
Do you realize that we had not been there together
since we toured in "Rio Rita"? However, I think we
could have even gone to the smelting operation in
Rockdale, TX and had fun.

Gallatoire's is so fabulous, and you know how we
enjoy cafe society - being able to walk straight to
our table and not even look at anyone. The way the
cherries jubilee desserts were flambeed in the dim
of candlelight was magnificent.

Maude, please don't go on one of those fad diets
again. You have no idea how well a bit of weight
becomes you - and not even a wrinkle.

I looked all over our grand bathroom suite at the
Hotel Monteleone to find what you are using, and I
could not find anything, but gold eye shadow. Now
what is it that you are wearing?

I adore you, Maude.

Millie

[27]Peggy Hopkins Joyce was an original and
infamous gold digger and she played one in the
movie, "International House". She broke the hearts
of her paramours and she married millionaires. If
one goes to the Smithsonian Institute one can see
the Portuguese Diamond she owned that is on
permanent display at the institute.

Dear Maude:

That damn Schyler has been worrying me to death.
His wife just had a baby, and can you believe he
wants to me to go out to a movie with him. I do
not want to offend him because he's such a nut.

He might do something wild like telling the office
manager my real name is Peggy Hopkins[27] Joyce, the
gold digger. Such scandalous news would just ruin
my career.

Neiman's delivered my new things. They fit beauti-
fully, but where will I wear them? I always end
up wearing cocktail suits instead of basic business
suits. I really must get social, but it's such a
bore to do so in Dallas.

I have not heard a word from Ms. H. She may have
been drowned on the Eastern Sea-board.

Please write.

Millicent

Dear Maude:

Don't ever undersell the providences, my dear. Last
weekend I just had to get away, and I ginned over
to Mineral Wells. Well, I returned to the Land of
Cowpokes absolutely exhausted from my activities.

I can't understand how you can sit there and
pretend to be the Louella Parsons of East Texas
if you don't write your copy. My copy of several
months ago has not been answered as of yet. I am
livid enough to sell you down the river socially.

Now what have you been doing, you glamorous thing?
Parties, cocktails, men and feathers they are the
story of your life. You are the wildest debutante
I know.

The conventions here have started up again which
means that the rich egg and butter crowd will be
in town. And, they are just grand!

Do write. Give my regards to Roger. Pinch his tit.
Is it true that Roger is really Natalie Wood in
drag?

Love,

Millie

Dear Maude:

I had a rather unusual affair from Shawnee,
Oklahoma a few days ago. They are not as
backward as one might expect.

Anyway, I am now an official American Indian
Princess.

Speaking of Oklahoma, the wildest, only wildest
weekend in Dallas is the Texas and Oklahoma game
in October. I think it would be so double ginger
peachy if you rigged up one of your glamorous hat
creations (no lampshades, please) and hurried down
from Houston to go to the game.

Bring along two oil daddies with you if you like.

Nothing happens at the game, but the NIGHT is the
hour and it is sort of like Mardis Gras. Think it
over and let me know. Or, if you insist on
going to the Game (I do know your weakness for
big things) I will find two raccoon coats for us.
We'll yell and scream in them, and we can take
turns applying Swedish massages to the teams.

Write.

Millie

Dear Maudine:

I wish you could come down here for a spell.

But, darling, I know you so very well. You are
one of those fancy, money making queens who think
only of their Louis XIV furniture and Dresden
bric-a-brac. And, of course, watercress and cucum-
ber sandwiches for tea. Nevertheless, I adore you.

Well, things are rolling at work - have made many
boo-boos, but I try to look as bewildered as Marie
Wilson when anything goes wrong.

My boss is out a great deal inspecting those big
boilermakers in the field. I try to dress plainly
and conservatively at the office, but the Chanel
socks are a dead giveaway.

After sitting nightly and rotting at home, rest
assured I will be putting on those party pumps
this Saturday night. I must get out.

My dear, after teaching last Saturday, I drove
home to Cow Town for the East Texas Flood. It was
impossible. I just knew I would be swept off the
highway and drowned in my car and there I was in
my old Bergdorf negligee.

Anyway, I am still alive. And I have a smile and I
still have a wiggle in my ass so I won't mope over
what might or could have happened.

By the way I wrote to Lois. She's a perfect bitch,
but actually had it not been for Lois I wouldn't

have met half the people I did.   Of course they
were all evil, but at least they had spirit.
Maude, there are times I wish I had stayed in
Hollywood even if it would have meant playing
comedy.

Millicent

Dearest Maudine:

You silly, flippant East Texas whore. It was
absolutely grand finally getting a note from you.
My dear, you can't fool Millie. I know what's been
going on. All of your spare time has been spent
tinting your egg costume for the Easter
festivities. You should be horse-whipped.

Saturday night I was ginning around when a damned
little bitch from SMU plows into my car and honey,
what that child did to my fender and lights would
melt the heart of a butch mechanic. I am so
terribly lucky having been born under Capricorn.

Now comes a little gem - I'm working again. I am
an assistant to a contractor from NY. I'm the office staff, and I don't have the faintest idea what
these truckers and these boilermakers are doing.
I type payrolls, check customer orders and do my
nails when opportunity affords. God, this blonde
wig is hot!

I had a Christmas card from Lois perched on
a Louis XIV chair at her Sutton Place home.
Alongside her chair was her pet Yorky.

I am sort of estranged from all of my New York
friends. Is there something I should know? My
friends are dropping me as someone would an
oversexed cobra.

Millie

Dear Maudine:

Thank you so much for that fabulous chin strap.
It was so thoughtful of you. After wearing it
only one night I look ten - well maybe five year
younger.

Did it really come from Paris? You are a big
darling. I have told the photographers that I am
ready for my close up before I start to sag again.
What is the scene?

You know how Parisian I am!

I tried out my new face at the bars and it was
your kind of evening. One was terribly athletic and
had just come from the gym. He was hung like a 13
pound ham, but he smelled like camel dung after
sunset. The runner up was in skin tight briefs
and he looked as prodigious as a peanut.

At the truck stops, we would call it a goober, but
take it from me some of these little ones can turn
into monsters.

All my devotion,

Love,

Millie

[28]Tall for an actress of the time (the Depression)
Connie Francis was a top femme fatale star
starring in over 60 films in 17 years. Unfortunately,
Warner Brothers began to give her B-movies. She
reportedly had affairs with both men and women.
Once, years after her career had dimmed, it is said
that Kay encountered her former Warner Brothers'
rival, Bette Davis. When Bette asked why Francis
had tolerated such abuse from Jack Warner,
Kay responded, "I didn`t give a damn.
I wanted the money." Davis commented,
"I didn`t. I wanted the career."

[29]It is said that Nat King Cole faced racial
persecution all of his life, even in Hollywood. He
began as a jazz pianist, but during the 1950's he
had many hit records of the likes of Frank Sinatra.
His "The Nat King Cole Show" produced in 1956
showcased wonderful talent such as Peggy Lee,
but there was little advertising sponsorship
for the show to succeed.

Dear Maudine:

Your phone call shook me right out of my chemise.
It was good to hear your voice again. You still
sound like Kay Francis[28].

Well, child, I am thriving on this office crap.
I simply adore Mr. and Mrs. Green, and they
absolutely worship me. Seriously, they are so
nice. And, they are chic and you know how much
that means to me.

The only fly in the ointment so to speak of has
been my bottom. Child, it is a real mess. I have
suffered more than Joan Crawford ever dare, and I
never know when I can whirl on a bar stool. And,
those damn bullets known in the medical profession
as suppositories are what keep me going. Can one
still get opium suppositories direct from Paris?

I hear that Ms. H. is still married in Peekskill.
She is probably putting up plum jelly like crazy.
I might send Lois a cashmere toilet seat cover for
Christmas.

I spend most of my weekends getting a gorgeous tan.
And, I am going to bleach my hair to glisten like
Nat King Cole's[29] teeth.

Love,

Millie

Dear Maude:

Your letter was better than the family size bottle
of Geritol. How I wish I could have been on the
streets with you in San Francisco. I am certain
that you are trying on all of the lovely things
you bought there.

I was in the hospital for eleven days, but only
because I fell in love with my doctor and refused
to be released. Without going into the gruesome
details the first movement after surgery is no
picnic, but I just pretended that it was gold coming
out. I can't as of yet do the harmonica trick. I just
don't have the musical education for it.

I have read that New York has changed so much.
We would not know it. Everything old is being
torn down. Incidentally, is it really true that
Lois Le Chance has bought the Empire State for
his cocktail parties, and he is making a duplex of
the Chrysler Building?

Have you seen the just released movie, "Gigi"? It
is just (I hate this word) divine. Louis Jourdan is
very disconcerting though. Throughout the movie
he flaunts a basket as big as the Ritz. I never did
touch my popcorn.

Millie

Dear Maude:

Halloween was sort of spinsterish. I had dinner
with a friend of Bill's, and we all played bridge
and then more bridge. Nick, the bartender at
Adolphus, is going to be livid with me. I had
promised I would show up in my costume - this
year it was to be a pregnant ballerina, but I
did not have time to whip it up.

My boss has been in Utah and he returned today.
I have worked twice as hard during his absence
trying to charm all of the various sales
representatives from Alcoa and other firms.

My heart was really broken yesterday when a
precious man from Reynolds Metals informed
me of his impending transfer to Chicago, Illinois.

When I heard this I just slammed my typewriter and
put my head on my desk and bawled.

Oh well, I can't even remember his name now so it
must not have been real love.

Stop polishing those tiaras and write.

Love,

Millie

[30]Anna May Wong is a gay diva who was marginalized in the 1950's in much the same way as gay men had been marginalized socially. She was fashionable in her costumes and she excelled in her roles, especially playing alongside Marlene Dietrich in "Shanghai Express", 1932. Although she was born an American in Los Angeles she was excluded from kissing Caucasian leading men and often lost Asian roles to Caucasian actresses.

[31]The WAMPAS Baby Stars was a promotional campaign and a awards ceremony for thirteen selected starlets of great promise made annually by The Western Association of Motion Picture Advertisers from 1922 to 1934 (although no baby stars were selected for years 1930 and 1933) respectively for the 1929 Great Stock Market Collapse and interference from the studios in 1933. It was a big year in 1926 with awards going to Joan Crawford, Delores del Rio, Fay Wray, Janet Gaynor and Mary Astor.

Dear Maude:

Your Christmas card was the most elegant and
elaborate thing I have seen since Grand Mama had
Mainbocher do our Easter dresses back during the
Depression. Seriously, your card was beautiful.

I woke up yesterday with a damn case of pleurisy.
Last night I could hardly breathe. I thought I was
going to the deep beyond and I suddenly remembered
I was 3 - I mean 28 and it was my birthday and I
just absolutely refused to die.

My place is coming along quite well. In case
you have not read my letters the decor is sort
of Oriental motif, very early Anna Mae Wong[30].
Frankly, my dear, if I see one more Shoji
screen, or another silk print I will die.

I am stuck with this, and next year I may go stark
raving French provincial. I am most anxious for
you to come up and advise me on the interior.

I just don't know what happened to my life. Remember when Hal Roach announced us as the brightest
of the Wampus Baby Stars[31], and then we dashed to
Europe because you felt Hollywood was cheap. Now,
I can't even get a decent part in the Lassie series.
I may work out a number with those wax bananas to
make a little money New Years.

Cora Sue Collins

[32]Jessica Dragonnette was a singer who performed operettas and classics for over 20 years. As Marlene Dietrich did she performed in USO activities and was also honored as a honorary colonel for her support of the enlisted troops.

[33]Nancy Gates was under contract with RKO when she was just 15, and her first movie was "Hitler's Children". She starred in movies from the 40's until the 50' and 60's. She was in comedies ("The Great Gildersleeve") and in Westerns and some science fiction films. She also had interesting appearances in some of the popular television shows.

Dear Jessica Dragonette[32]:

What a drag (if you'll pardon the expression) this place is. Mrs. Green has been on a jewel buying spree, and we have been combing jewelers. Today, she bought a 44 carat topaz and it looks grand on me.

My job is hectic, but Maudine I think I have found myself. Of course, sometimes I get so furious with this life I go to the men's room and do three pirouettes.

Doesn't Schyler know when she is frozen? He is such a nut. And, after what you told me I'm afraid to be too nasty as he might try to slash my breasts or something. I simply do not enjoy psychopathic people.

Ms. Harold (his little tea party with the young enlistee may be over) might come to TX. Darling, do you have any rich friends who could afford him, or do you know of any library needing an attractive spinster with a tart tongue?

I am going to a picnic tonight with my cousin and her congenial mad friends. I do adore picnics. It always makes me think of those lovely Sundays in Salina, Kansas when you and I used to picnic and motor boat. Remember when I fell out of the boat - I suspect you pushed me.

Love,

Nancy Gates[33]

[34]Natalie Wood played Marjorie in the film, "Marjorie Morningstar". Herman Wouk's book of a Jewish girl coming of age was a best seller in the 1950's and it was brought to film in 1958.

[35]Joan Crawford was born Louise LeSueur. She reportedly once said, "I love playing bitches. There is a lot of bitch in every woman – a lot in every man". She had a rough life amongst classmates' taunts when she attended Stephen's College. She had to work on campus to pay for her tuition and books. One of Hollywood's most successful actresses and toughest she suffered a low period, but she came on top again with her academy award- winning "Mildred Pierce" in 1945. It has been said (true or not) that upon learning of Crawford's death in 1977 Bette Davis remarked "the bitch always was on time". She married Pepsi-Cola Company Chairman, Alfred Steele, at the home of former actor William Haines and his partner. It is said that William Haines was the first openly gay actor who left Hollywood at his discretion. He turned his creativity to interior design and furniture design.

Dear Marjorie Morningstar[34]:

Please fasten your safety belt. I had a letter
from Ms. Harold who was vacationing on Fire Island.
Would you believe she had a place there for the
summer close to Lois Le Chance's cottage?

Ms. H. and Lois had sort of reconciliation on the
island; and, Lois threw a huge Texas theme party
for over 300 guests. She had two, 20 foot lighted
oil derricks in front of her little shack in the
Grove.

There were 1,000 cases of champagne and Ms. H. said
that there was enough champagne on hand for three
Lawrence Welk orchestras.

Isn't that so like Lois Le Chance? Bless her heart,
she is sweet, but I have always thought of her as
being a bit on the vulgar side.

All my devotion,

Lucille LeSeur[35]

[36]Earl Wilson, the New York columnist, said "last night Tallulah Bankhead barged down the aisle as Cleopatra and sank". Her father was the democratic Speaker of the U.S. House of Representatives. Known for her husky voice she was a party girl with a sexual appetite for both men and women reportedly including Marlene, Joan Crawford and other female stars. "Dahlings, I was wonderful" she exclaimed when presented the New York Film Critics Circle award for her outstanding performance in "Lifeboat".

[37]An actor, Charles Laughton, Jr., also directed "The Night of the Hunter" which is considered a critical masterpiece of the 1950's that starred Lillian Gish, Robert Mitchum and Shelley Winters. He had a superb voice to lend to his one-man reading tours. In his wife's (Elsa Lancaster) memoir she said that the couple never had children because he was homosexual.

Dear Maude:

It's Saturday evening. Can you believe that I have
a ghastly cold (no dear I wasn't doing it with anyone under a pine tree), and my voice is sort of a
cross between Bankhead's[36] and Charles Laughton's[37].
That should prove a fabulous combination in the
bistro this evening.

I feel too badly to go out, but what the hell,
Maude, as long as they sell it I am going to
buy it.

My long Christmas was kaput. I had to come back
to a dance teachers' convention and it was so dull.
Holly Pritchard (the old bag from Houston) saw the
president of the association making over me. I
completely ignored her. And, honey, I had that
convention going my way.

Well, this will kill you. Ms. H. is still with her
young New Jersey lover and living in a bowl of
domesticity. I can never seem to get my life that
complicated.

Do get up here. Any weekend is fine. Just pack
those tweezers and your chin strap and roll.

Darling, I must get out of this cot; drink some
orange juice, get gorgeous and get downtown. It
sounds provincial as hell.

Love to you,

Millie

[38]Helen Twelvetrees was an actress during the early talkies period. For the most part she was miscast and played the roles of women enduring the pain of being romantically involved with the wrong man. She reportedly committed suicide at the age of forty-five.

Dear Maudine:

I did appreciate your postcard from the enchanted
West Coast, and I complied with a hastily written
note to await your arrival. As usual, I have not a
word from you. I suppose I will get a Halloween
card from you in Trinidad.

Actually, I know what you have been doing. You
are running a smart hat shop on the ship channel
in Galena Park, Houston. Lucille Ball is raving
about one of your 42 pound creations. You have
always worked well with veils and sea shells.

I have done nothing all summer, but work and take
the sun on Sunday. I do make an effort to get
dressed on Saturday nights, and I then take in a
few bars merely for reasons of noblesse oblige. It
can at times be far from interesting. I try to be
very casual - all black, sweater, slacks, shoes and
a white shirt for the Newport, Rhode Island-Pat
Ward look. It does not always go over.

I did meet a most agreeable young person from (of
all places) Cisco, Texas. He said he is coming into
town tomorrow, and he is presenting me with a red
rose. I wrote a curt note back saying that although I would be available I was hardly the red
rose type. I prefer stocks and bonds.

Helen Twelvetrees[38]

Dear Maude:

Thank you for writing and confirming my suspicion about your hat making activities in Galena Park.

I can just see you on the channel doing the Handkerchief Dance with all of those drunken Greek sailors.

Do you prefer the ones with the big anchors in their pants?

I have always wanted to wear one of those Edwardian tea hats with glowing white egret feathers. You must try your hand designing with egrets, if you haven't already.

I have been taking opium suppositories once a month for my sinuses.

I adore you.

Love,

Millie

Dear Maude:

Do you realize that I am almost 29 years of age and I have never ever been married? I don't count my first two lovers.

Everyone is so worried about my married status, including my boss's wife.

If I could find a nice, congenial rich girl I think I might be tempted to try marriage. As Mehitable said, "Hell, I'll try any kind of marriage".

Doll, I have to go, that adorable Neiman Marcus delivery boy is driving up with some gorgeous shirts and slacks I ordered yesterday, and I think I will serve him a coke for his courtesy.

Child, about two weeks ago, I looked in my closet, and I noticed that some vile person had come in and made way with some of my lovely Neiman numbers. I had to go out and buy more. What else could I do?

Let me know if Paris calls.

Love,

Millicent

[39]Jeanette MacDonald and Nelson Eddy, Hollywood's romantic on-screen pair in many movies from the early 1930's to the 1940's , were romantically involved although she married actor Gene Raymond. It is said that MacDonald and Raymond divorced after he was arrested in a raid on a West Hollywood gay bar. She never won an Oscar, but she was an immense star for MGM.

Dearest Maudine:

Instead of staying home Friday night playing my
Jeannette McDonald/Nelson Eddy[39] records and living
the life of an aging courtesan, I ventured down
to "Adolphus" bar. I might as well have been in
Sullivan's Drugstore in Centerville, Texas.

I was so glamorous, and I was so alone there.
But darling, any day now I may be returning to
Hollywood. They want to do my life story up to
1942.

Maude, please haul ass and come up. I am so
lonely and weary, I could just die. I am so bored
with these cheap Dallas queens. And, you know how
much I enjoy stimulating people, smart places, good
music, good food and most any type of man.

Now, just don't say you will come and then make all
kinds of excuses for not visiting such as going on
a Jamaica honeymoon.

Maude, I adore you, and you make my life brighter.

Love,

Millie

Dear Maude:

I know that this is the petit point season for you, but honey I do wish I had your shoulder to weep on.

I have gone through the most tragic romance of this, or any year.

At first it seemed to me as if that little bluebird of happiness had entered my dreary life to bring the eternal love we all long for. However, the little bluebird only shit on me.

Now, one hot evening, I was running around in my MG pretending I was Connie Bennett[40]. Lo and behold, this blue Thunderbird began following me (you know we are not permitted to wave at them), and then the T-Bird stops alongside my car. A voice says, "Come ride with me".

I said, "No, you ride with me". Darling, six feet of the loveliest male specimen you have ever seen emerged and wedged it in my little car.

We rode and shortly we took a detour to my apartment. It was heaven (as Ginger Rogers[41] used to sing). He was 30, a surgeon with lots of money, a gorgeous apartment and he was a most charming attractive person.

I immediately put on the Boston debutante act and it went well. A few days later another call and then a surprise visit and more calls and it was too divine for words.

This was the most complete affair I have ever had. Then, Saturday when I was supposed to be at

his apartment in ten minutes, I was detained by a
former hotel jerk that I discarded weeks earlier.
Nothing happened, but I think the doctor smelled a
rat and took a ride around the block.

Bang, I have been treated like a ragamufin. Maude,
I am so torn up I could just die and never, never
make another picture.   I had no friends to talk to
and no one to cheer me up, or to say, "Millie you
must stop this".

Now, that is enough of my tragic, sordid life in
Texas. I am leaving this Friday to spend a few
days at the strand in Galveston. Nothing is
really planned. I may even just drive on right
into the Gulf of Mexico and let the starfish eat
me up. I have to have time to sort of think things
out. I am just so distressed and upset. And, I am
sick that you are not coming here soon to visit.

I am also seriously tinkering with the idea of
going back into the circus.

Love,

Bozo

[40]Constance 'Connie' Bennett was born into an acting family and she
began her career in silent films, but following marriage and divorce she
resumed acting in the 'talkies'. She was a blond fashion plate in the early
1950's, but her career dwindled until she was cast in the 1960's movie,
"Madame X", where she played the mother of Holly Parker (Lana Turner).
She died shortly after the film at the age of 60.

[41]Ginger Rogers was a singer, comedic actress and, of course, Fred
Astaire's dance partner in "Flying Down to Rio" and "The Gay Divorcee"
among several RKO musicals of the 1930's. She always played happy, vi-
vacious roles, but she won an Academy Award for Best Actress in her less
light-hearted role in "Kitty Foyle". She lived in the Palm Springs, California
neighboring community of Rancho Mirage until her death in 1995 from
congestive heart failure.

[42]James Dean's success happened so fast in the movies that he and his career leaped over the pack. He was immediately nominated for Best Actor in Steinbeck's "East of Eden". Two other movies "Rebel Without a Cause" and "Giant" had not been released by the time of his tragic death in a car accident in 1955. His legacy is both a cinematic as well as a commercial legacy especially with the iconic posters that capture the ambivalent look of youth. Dean, it is reported, was bisexual.

Dear Maudine:

I was just ready to go jump into Galveston Bay
nude (except for some little beach jewelry) when
your note arrived. It was like a sprig of spring
heather.

Honey, if I were not so gay I would have blown
(yes) my brains out by now. Since my disastrous
love affair I have new agents, the Abels. There
is the opportunity to teach at a new ballet school.

The studio is lush, air-conditioned and the ballet
studio is a dream - pink walls, mirrors galore and
a autographed picture of James Dean[42]. The Abels
say they will spare no expense in advertising me.

I just want to be a world famous dancer. Oh,
Maudine we should have never left New York,
for after all, happiness is a thing with lights.

Do you think we're too old to make another
debut somewhere? If we just had a Spanish shawl
we could do fine here. I have met the Texas
press, interviewed on radio and I have done
everything, but do a strip tease in the Driskill
Hotel (I don't have the tits for it).

I just don't understand this material life.

Love,

Millicent

Dear Eula Faye:

Mary, what have I done? The Abels called me several times to reconsider their offer. I did reconsider and I accepted. I am now at the ballet school which is lovely and air-conditioned as I mentioned.

Enrollment will likely be slim at first due to late advertising. I am on a 45% gross, and if things go well then it will be nice. Classes begin tomorrow and I hope in two months to have 150 students. If not then I may dump all the crinolines in the backseat of the car, and I will drive somewhere, maybe Buda.

Now don't get panicky if this does not work. I am not going to barge in on you with my old makeup box or defeated furs.

I want to be fair to the Abels, but I just can't sit around waiting too long for things to happen, or to be profitable as I have most of my life. I am so tired of living like a gypsy.

I have a small, cute apartment that I have temporarily rented. I believe that they are called guest houses. It is back off of this Norma Desmond Sunset Boulevard[43] type home. There is a swimming pool which lies right outside my kitchen window for my view. The place is littered with life size cherubs and sculptures, moats and flagstone steps; and I am up to my waist in thick, dark green ivy. I want you to visit.

I appeared on an interview on the Ruth Sullivan radio show. She is the Arlene Francis of East Texas. I have several television things scheduled as well.

I am also working with a wonderful girl at the
dance studio who has studied in New York, and she
knows the difference between camp and straight. She
is a joy, and we have one routine worked out together. We will probably perform it on television
next week. Really, she is like a breath of fresh
spring air.

And, I am giving a private lesson to a boy who is
fifteen years old. I am afraid he will be headed
soon for the primrose bushes, as you well know
what I mean. Don't worry! I loathe chicken.

Please come and see me at once. I have a wonderful
new Simmons mattress, and we can camp on it until the boats come in. Now, don't back out with your
usual excuses such as lock-jaw. Just say, I am
going to see Millie and do it.

I need your moral support.

Love,

Millie

[43]Gloria Swanson played Norma Desmond in "Sunset Boulevard" a role
she was destined to play as the tragic, aging silent screen star of this
classic movie. She was the actress who could deliver the immortal
Norma and the many memorable lines in the movie. "I am big. It's the
pictures that got small" is just one of the memorable quotes of the movie.
Pola Negri declined the role saying she was too tired, and Mae West, at
age 56, declined the role as well stating that first of all she was not old. It
is said that Mae West went to Las Vegas instead to perform with her male
muscle boy revue.

[44]Tab Hunter, a 50's heartthrob, was blond and handsomely youthful; and later admitted his homosexuality in his autobiography, "Tab Hunter Confidential: The Making of a Movie Star". In his autobiography, Hunter speaks to the rumor that his and Rory Calhoun's agent sacrificed them to "Confidential" Magazine in order to protect Rock Hudson's career. Once to Hunter's chagrin Tallulah "blurted to some reporter during a rehearsal, Tab must be gay - he hasn't gone down on me!" "Young Love", recorded by Hunter in 1956, became Billboard's number one hit. He is also known for his role in the cult-classic "Lust in the Dust".

[45]Margaret O'Brien began work as a child actress in a number of movies and later starred alongside Judy Garland as 'Tootie' in "Meet Me in St. Louis", a 1944 MGM musical, and also appeared in "Little Women". She gives speaking engagements about her career and is a resident of the Palm Springs, California area.

Dear Maude:

What a relief to get your note! I heard you had
gone to Hollywood to testify for the movie tabloids
regarding Tab Hunter[44] and Margaret O'Brien[45].

Ma Chere, I must tell you first. The ballet
studio deal fell through. Our enrollment was too
slim, and then what students I had came down with
influenza including my accompanist. It was a
disaster. I thought for certain that we would have
to go through quarantine. And, the story goes on.

The count simply will not leave me alone, and he
has invited me to join him for the fall at his new
pied-a-terre at Champs de Mars near the Eiffel
Tower. He is so jealous, and he wants me all to
himself. I am going to let him wait on me like a
Russian princess which I am actually.

He is christening the yacht, The Millicent.

I cannot write for awhile. Do you still like large
stones? Rubies or diamonds, which are the more
expensive? We still have a few good years left,
don't we?

Love,

Millie (Capucine)

www.ingramcontent.com/pod-product-compliance
Lightning Source LLC
Chambersburg PA
CBHW070852280326
41934CB00008B/1407